No More Secrets
for Me

No More Secrets for Me

For Me

Sexual Abuse Is a Secret No Child
Should Have to Keep!

by Oralee Wachter

Illustrated by Jane Aaron

Cover illustration by Michael Emberley

 Little, Brown and Company
Boston New York London

To my grandchildren—
Olivia, Zachary, Becky, Jason, Natalie, and Ben,
and to all my children

Revised Edition

Library of Congress Cataloging-in-Publication Data

Wachter, Oralee.
    No more secrets for me.
    Summary: In four separate stories on the theme of sexual abuse of children, young victims are able to articulate their feelings and defend themselves, often with the help of another person whom they trust.
ISBN 0-316-88290-9 (hc)
ISBN 0-316-99042-6 (pb)
    1. Children's stories, American. [1. Child molesting — Fiction. 2. Short Stories]
I. Aaron, Jane, ill. II. Title.
PZ7.W1134No 1983 [Fic]   83-12077

10 9 8 7 6 5 4 3 2 1

WOR

Printed in the United States of America

About this edition:

No More Secrets for Me was first published in 1983. It's being released again because today, like then, there is widespread concern about preventing the sexual abuse of children. Recently, there have been front-page articles about the molestation of children by adults who take advantage of their power and position. Whether or not child sexual abuse makes the headlines, the challenge is the same as it was twenty years ago: to help children protect themselves from adults who prey on them.

No More Secrets for Me is a book of stories to read with children. Each story centers around a common example of abuse to help children discriminate about whom they can trust, how to avoid potential abuse, and how to tell an adult about abuse that may have already taken place.

If you are approached by a child for help, be aware that every state has laws protecting children from sexual abuse. Call the Child Protective Services agency in your state to assist a child who may come to you for help. These numbers are listed in the front pages of all telephone directories. There is also a resource guide in the back of this book.

INTRODUCTION

It's NOT FAIR, but it happens. Someone you know, or someone you like, or someone in your family touches you, and you don't like it. It doesn't feel good the way hugging and holding hands does. It isn't fun like wrestling. It doesn't feel close and comfortable the way it does when someone you love puts an arm around you.

If someone touches your body in a way you don't like, you may feel mixed up. You may feel as if you were tricked or forced into it. Or maybe the person makes you promise not to tell anyone and to keep the touching a secret. This book is about taking care of yourself, just in case this ever happens to you or to a friend.

"Talking Helps" introduces the basic ideas of privacy and personal boundaries to very young children. Adults often know when something doesn't feel right, and children do too. Encourage them to identify and trust their feelings, and to tell you right away if anyone touches them in a way they don't like. Tell them: "Your body belongs to you. If anyone touches you in a way you don't like, it's OK to tell them you don't like it. And tell me too and I will tell them to stop it." This is the most important information you can give a child.

TALKING HELPS

DARRYL came home drenched from the rain. Terrie, the baby-sitter, was there waiting for him. She came over every day to keep an eye on him until his mom got home from work.

"Hi, Darryl," she said. "Take off your raincoat. You're dripping all over the place."

He took his homework papers out of the pocket of his slicker and looked at the watery purple ink. The wad of wet ditto papers was definitely too faded to read. No homework today, he thought.

"You're soaked," Terrie said. "How about a bath to warm you up?"

Darryl was surprised. Usually they had a snack.

"A bath," he protested. "How come? I'm wet enough."

Terrie was already in the bathroom running the water. She pulled off his sweater and was about to pull down his jeans when the phone rang. Terrie went to answer it.

"I can take my own clothes off," Darryl said to himself. He closed the door, got undressed, and slid down into the warm water. It felt good. He knew Terrie was talking to her boyfriend, Robert. They talked for a long time every day.

Terrie hung up the phone and called out. "Darryl. Pull out the plug before the water gets cold."

A minute later she walked right into the bathroom. She grabbed a towel, wrapped him up, and started to dry him off.

"Don't, Terrie. I'll do it myself. Go wait for me in the kitchen," Darryl said.

Terrie looked at him for a minute and laughed.
"Darryl, I bet you're embarrassed, aren't you? Just

because you're naked. That's silly. I know all about boys. I've got two brothers, you know. They run around the house half undressed all the time. It's no big deal."

Without waiting for him to answer, she finished drying him all over. Even his bottom.

"It's a big deal to me, Terrie. I don't like it."

When his mother got home he was still in a bad mood. "I don't want Terrie to baby-sit me anymore," he announced.

"Why not?" asked his mother. "I thought you liked her."

Darryl was confused. He didn't know what to say. Darryl did like Terrie, except for one thing. She always kept an eye on him, even when he didn't want her to. She never knocked on the door to the bathroom. She didn't let him get dressed by himself.

His mother put her arm around him and hugged him. "Talk to me, Darryl. If something's

bothering you, I want to know what it is. Maybe I can help."

"Well," he started out, "I don't like Terrie to undress me. I don't like her to dry me off, either. I don't want her to walk in all the time when I'm in the bathtub."

"I can understand that," answered his mother. "Have you ever told her how you feel?"

"It doesn't do any good," he said. "She won't listen to me. She says I'm just being silly. Can't you get another baby-sitter?"

"Sure I can, Darryl," said his mother. "If we can't get Terrie to listen to you and respect your feelings, I will look for someone else. But first I'd like to talk to her and explain."

"What will you say?" asked Darryl.

"I'll say something like, 'Darryl and I want you to baby-sit. But only if you pay attention to his feelings. That means listening to him and respecting his privacy about his body.' How does that sound?"

"Pretty dumb. She won't listen."

"We don't know that, Darryl, until we try. I'll talk to her tonight."

The next day when Darryl came home from school, Terrie was there, as usual, doing her homework in the kitchen. "Got any homework today?" she asked.

"Yeah. Spelling."

"Let's make some popcorn first. Then I'll quiz you. Okay?"

"Sure," said Darryl.

Terrie poured oil into the black frying pan. Darryl spilled in the corn. He put on the lid. She turned on the flame.

"Guess what?" said Terrie.

"What?" answered Darryl.

"Your mom and I had a talk. I guess I didn't understand how you felt about some things."

The first kernels started to pop. Darryl slid the heavy pan back and forth over the flame. He felt funny talking about it.

"From now on I'll be more careful. I won't embarrass you anymore. Okay?"

"Okay," said Darryl. All the corn was popping at once. "It's your turn, Terrie. My hand's getting tired."

"Right," said Terrie. "I'm glad to help."

This story reveals how easy it is for a "friendly" adult to shake the confidence of a young person. It also makes clear that it is not OK for someone to trick you, scare you, or promise you things to make you do something you don't want to do. That is the next piece of information a child needs.

JUST IN CASE

ON SATURDAY MORNING, Nickie cleaned up her room. She took the sheets off the bed and carried them down to the washing machine. Before she stuffed them in, she ran her hand around inside the bottom of the machine, just in case. She felt a thin coin and slid it over to a drain hole and picked it up. A lucky sign, she thought, and put the dime in her pocket.

Back in her room, Nickie picked up a week's worth of clothes. She went through all her pockets and tossed the change she had collected on the mattress. A dollar thirty-seven. That's enough for four, maybe five, video games, if she didn't buy a soda.

Nickie loved video games. She looked forward to playing every Saturday at Stoney's.

"Bye, Mom. I'm going," she said on her way out.

"Did you finish your room?"

"Yeah. Spick and span. See you later." Then she added, just in case, "Can I have a dollar?"

Her mother smiled at the familiar routine. "Nope," she said.

"Fifty cents?" asked Nickie. "I'm really getting good."

Her mother shook her head. She knew Nickie was determined to get a high score and put her initials on the video screen.

"I'll be the first girl to do it. Nickie Owens. Right up there next to GGG. He thinks he's so great."

"Not with my money, though," said her mom.

Nickie gave it one last try. "Mom, one little tiny quarter?"

"N for Nickie, O —"

"For Owens, *no.*" Nickie finished the sentence. She had heard it enough to know it was no use. "I'll be back by five. See ya."

None of her friends were at Stoney's when she got there, except for good old Gus.

"Hello, Nickie," he said. "How come you're here so early?"

"Hi, Mr. Tresant," she said.

Everyone knew Gus. He used to be a music

teacher, but now he spent most of his time at Stoney's, talking to the kids. He tried to be friendly. Sometimes he'd buy everyone sodas or a pizza. Some of the kids teased him behind his back, but Nickie felt sorry for him. One time he told her that she reminded him of his granddaughter, who had moved away.

"Today's my lucky day. I'm going to make it into the top ten."

"I know you can do it, Nickie," he said, smiling at her. "Here's a quarter — have a game on me."

"No, that's okay," she said. "I've got money."

Nickie dropped in a quarter and looked at the scoreboard. TOP 10 SCORES: REY TWP MT MEK WSL SFH VB PKC ACR GGG. The GGG stood for Gordy "The Great" Glaser. She was concentrating on her game when Gordy, Kevin, and some of her friends came in. She was up to 32,500 and things were moving fast. Oops. Bleep. She lost it.

"You finished?" asked Gordy.

"No," she answered. "Not yet."

"C'mon," he said. "You'll never make it, Nickie."

Nickie kept playing. Kevin and Gordy stood next to her watching every move she made. "Watch out, above, left, left, whoa!" Then suddenly — GAME OVER: SCORE 68,000. Wow! Good, but not good enough.

"What did I tell ya?" said Gordy.

"Yeah," added Kevin, "you're just wasting your time."

Gordy edged in front of her and took over the game. "You through?" he asked.

He was already playing by the time Nickie said, "Yeah, go ahead."

Nickie slumped down with her friends at the corner booth. "Can I have some?" she asked, reaching for Judy's can of soda. "I almost made it that time."

Judy pushed her soda over to Nickie. "We're going to see *E. T.* You want to go?"

"Again?" asked Nickie. "We've already seen it twice, and anyway, I don't have enough money."

"I'll lend you the money. C'mon with us, Nickie."

"No, I better not."

Judy just looked at her. "Okay. I guess I'll see you later."

Sitting alone in the booth, she heard cheering coming from the video game in the corner. She knew without looking that Gordy had just won another game. "I might as well go home," she thought. "No use in hanging around here."

"What's the matter, Nickie?" It was Gus. "Come here and sit down a minute." He patted the seat next to him. "How about a soda?"

"Okay." Nickie sat down on the other side of the booth.

Gus bought a can of soda and sat down beside

her. "If you don't want to come over to my side," he said, "I'll come over to yours. Tell me what's wrong — you look downhearted."

"It's not my lucky day after all," she said. "I didn't get into the top ten scores."

Gus moved closer to her and put his arm around her. "That's not such a big problem, Nickie," he said. "You just need to practice. Here's some extra change for you. Go ahead."

Nickie looked at the quarters on the table and at Mr. Tresant's face smiling at her. It wasn't really a warm, friendly smile. "It's okay, Nickie. You can take the money," he said. "I like all the kids, but you're my favorite."

Suddenly she had a funny feeling. She didn't like his arm around her, even if he was old Gus. She didn't feel sorry for him anymore. She wanted to get out and get away from him. Nickie tried to squirm out of his reach. "I have to go home now, Mr. Tresant. Let me out."

"But you didn't drink your soda," he said. "Don't be in such a hurry."

"I don't want it. I don't want the money. I want to go now," said Nickie, as Mr. Tresant moved a little closer to her.

"But don't you want to play . . ."

She didn't wait for him to finish the sentence. She slid down under the table and crawled up on the other side of the booth. "No," she said in a loud voice, and marched out the door.

"N for Nickie, O for Owens," she said over and over to herself on the long walk home. When she got there, her mother asked, "Well? Did you make it?"

"No. Not this time. But my initials came in handy anyway."

Nickie told her mother what had happened with Mr. Tresant. "I just got this icky feeling, Mom, when he put his arm around me. I wanted the quarters, but something felt wrong. I had to say no, just in case."

"I'm glad you had the gumption to tell him no and get out of there. He shouldn't be offering you money, and he has no business touching you or anyone else."

"What's gumption?"

"Gumption is when you don't like what's happening and you say so, loud enough for someone to hear you."

Nickie's mom hugged her. Nickie hugged her back. It felt so good to be hugged by someone she loved.

"What If…" takes place away from home—in summer camp—when children turn to their counselors for guidance and as role models. Children need help to separate and clarify their mixed feelings. Sometimes even people we like do things we don't like. Sometimes, things start out OK and then change. If this happens, it's OK to say no and to say stop. If it does not stop, children need to know it is not their fault, no matter what the situation is. Only the adult is responsible for abusive behavior.

WHAT IF...

GREG had never been to an overnight, sleep-away camp before. But here he was, a Badger for one week. According to his counselor Marty, the Badgers were certain to win the Good Sportsmanship Award, provided they were all good sports.

Greg liked both his counselors. Marty built a huge campfire every night and got it blazing with only one match. The kids called him "Matchless." Greg's other counselor was Vince. He could hit long fly balls to center field all day. He was a neat guy.

But there were a couple of things about camp that Greg didn't like. For one thing, he wasn't used to eating with so many people at the table, passing bowls of creamed corn and grabbing at

hot dogs. And, he didn't like getting undressed in front of everybody or taking showers with other kids, either. He hated to lend his soap and towel to Barry, who could never find his own things. But he did it to be a "good sport."

Every afternoon the Badgers went swimming. On Tuesday, Greg put on his swimsuit, but when everyone went down to the lake with Vince, he stayed behind. He wanted some peace and quiet. He flopped down on his bunk. It felt good to be alone in the cool, dark tent.

"Hey, Greg. Are you in there?" It was Marty, peeking in and squinting into the darkness. "What're you doing? Why aren't you down at the lake?"

"Can't I skip it today, Marty? I don't feel like swimming," answered Greg.

"What's wrong? You homesick or something?" Marty asked.

"Maybe, a little," Greg answered.

"I know how that is. Sometimes I get homesick myself, up here all summer," said Marty.

"You do?"

"Sure. I miss eating pizza and watching the games on TV. And Teddy."

"Who's Teddy?" asked Greg.

"Teddy's my dog," answered Marty. "He's my pal. He's a good old guy. He'd love to run around up here."

"How come you didn't bring him with you?"

"We're not supposed to; it's against the rules. *No dogs allowed.*" Marty sat down on the bunk next to Greg and said, "And you're not supposed to be in here, either. You know that, don't you, Greg?"

"I guess so."

"You could get in trouble if I told anyone. You know that?"

Greg nodded.

"But I know how you feel. Don't worry. I won't say anything. It's just between us. How's that?"

"Okay," answered Greg.

"Now, how about you doing something for me? How about a little game to cheer me up?"

"Sure," said Greg. "What do you want to play?"

Then Marty did a weird thing. He took off his bathing suit and T-shirt and sat down naked on Greg's bunk.

"First, take off your bathing suit. Then I'll show you the rest of the game," Marty said.

Greg thought it sounded like a stupid idea. He shook his head no.

"What are you afraid of?" teased Marty. "I'm not going to hurt you."

"Nothing," answered Greg. "I just don't want to, that's all."

Marty kept talking quietly. "It's just a game. I'm not going to do anything," he said.

"Then why should I take my clothes off?" said Greg, who was starting to feel very uncomfortable.

"I just want to look at you. C'mon, be a good sport."

"No," said Greg. He got off his bunk and held on to the top of his trunks.

"I guess I'll tell Vince that you skipped out on swimming," said Marty. "I bet he's going to be mad at you."

Greg felt trapped. Why was Marty doing this? He thought Marty was his friend. What kind of a trick was this anyway?

Greg dashed out of the tent and ran into the

woods near the lake. He could see Vince and the Badgers practicing lifesaving. He saw Marty go over to Vince and tell him something. Greg was scared. What were they saying? He could feel his heart pounding and tears coming into his eyes. He was still crying when Vince finally found him.

"Where have you been? I sent Marty to look for you," he said.

"He found me," said Greg, wiping his face and eyes. "I was just in the tent."

"What's wrong? What are you crying about?"

Greg didn't know whether to tell Vince what had happened or not. What if he got in trouble for being a bad sport? But, what if Marty tried to trick him like that again? He blurted out the story.

"It's about Marty," he said. "He told me to take off all my clothes. He said it was a game. He said I'd get in trouble if I didn't do what he said."

"Are you sure Marty did that?" Vince asked.

Greg nodded.

"Sometimes people do things that are hard to understand," Vince explained. "I'll talk to him and straighten this out, Greg."

Greg was still worried. He told Vince, "I don't want to get Marty in trouble."

"Listen, Greg. No one should trick you into playing a game that hurts your feelings. Or a game that you don't like. You did the right thing to tell me. And I don't want you to worry about it. That's my job. To help out. To solve problems. Okay?" said Vince. He took Greg's hand and waded a few feet into the lake.

"What's going to happen to Marty?" Greg asked.

"I don't know yet," answered Vince. "But that's Marty's problem, not yours. Your problem is catching up on Junior Lifesaving. Now jump in."

Greg felt relieved. He did a racing dive into the shallow water and swam out to the raft.

Maybe the Badgers wouldn't win the Good Sportsmanship Award this year, he thought. It didn't seem so important anymore.

Greg still didn't like to eat with so many people, or take showers with them, either. But he did earn his Junior Lifesaving badge. And most important, Greg found out he could say no and still be a pretty good sport. He thought about coming back next summer to practice catching long fly balls in center field.

In the vast majority of cases, children who are abused at home can't break out of this situation without adult help. Children need assurance that an adult will believe them and take action to see that the abuse is stopped.

PROMISE NOT TO TELL

MAUREEN put on her nightgown and got under the covers. It was still early, and she liked this time before going to sleep. At least she used to. This was her private time to do whatever she wanted. Tonight she had closed the door and turned on the radio. Now she took out her pack of felt markers to doodle and to write in her diary.

Maureen and her best friend, Beth, kept diaries. Beth called hers a journal. Sometimes they'd read pages to each other. Like the time Maureen read the part about when her mom and Pete got married last year and how she wondered what having a stepfather would be like. Or the time Beth read Maureen the part about her brother getting caught driving a car without a license. They told each other everything.

Then she heard Pete calling. "Maureen. Are you ready?" He was going to come up and tuck her in, as he called it. She used to like it when he sat on the bed and talked to her about school and gymnastics. He knew about backward rolls, walk-overs, and cartwheels. He had taught her how to play checkers when she had the chicken pox.

But now things were different. He did something he had never done before. He put his hands under the covers and touched her body. He said it was their special secret, and he made her promise never to tell anyone. She had promised.

Tonight when she heard his voice, Maureen scooped up her felt markers and diary and slid them under her pillow. She snapped off the light, pulled the blankets up over her head, and closed her eyes. She thought, "I'll pretend I'm asleep. Maybe he'll go away."

That didn't work. Pete opened the door and said quietly, "Maureen, I came to tuck you in. You like that, don't you?"

She lay as still as a stone. She couldn't open her mouth to say a word. She wanted to tell him no . . . please go away.

Pete sat down on the bed and pulled the covers down. He lifted her nightgown and touched her chest and her tummy and all over. She wanted to yank the covers up under her chin and tell him to

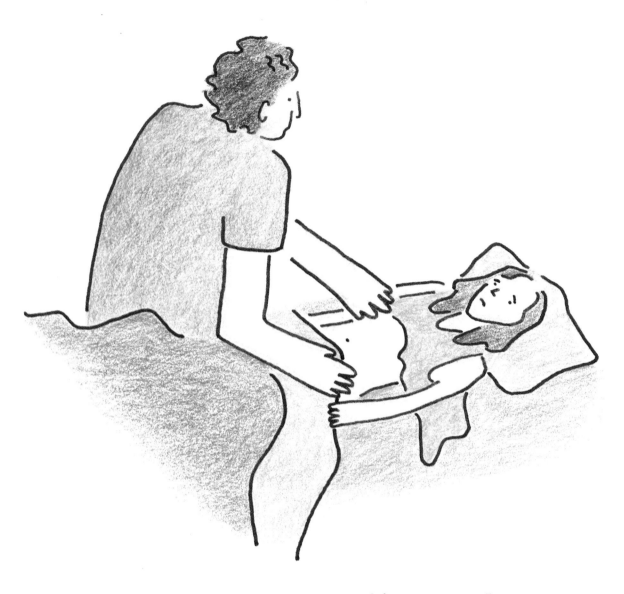

go away, to stop it. But she couldn't move. It was like being trapped in a nightmare.

Then Pete smoothed her nightie down, covered her up, and whispered, "Remember, honey, this is our little secret. Promise not to tell Mom or anyone."

Maureen felt terrible. She was mixed up and sad at the same time. Why was he doing this? Why was it a secret? she wondered. She needed someone to help her figure out what to do. Beth knew everything; maybe she could help.

After school the next day, Beth and Maureen walked through the park and played on the baby swings. They stood on the canvas baskets, taking turns twisting the chains into spirals and letting go, twirling and untwirling.

Maureen flopped down on the grass. "I'm dizzy," she said.

Nothing seemed to bother Beth, who rummaged around in her backpack for the apple she had saved from lunch. "Want a bite?"

"Ugh. No." answered Maureen.

Beth pulled out her journal. "I've got an entry to read to you."

Maureen listened as Beth read about a secret club at school. But her mind was on another secret.

"Beth," Maureen interrupted, "what would you do if you had a secret that was really awful?"

"Awful? Like what? Read it to me."

"It's not in my diary. I've never told anyone. I wouldn't dare write it down."

"Come on, Maureen. I tell you everything," said Beth.

"This is different. It's about Pete. It's a secret, and anyway, he made me promise not to tell."

"It's about Pete — your stepfather? What about him?"

"Sometimes when my mom is away, he comes into my room at night. He pretends to tuck me in . . ." Maureen closed her eyes. This was the hard part. "But he really wants to touch me under my nightgown," she said.

"You mean all over?" Beth asked.

Maureen looked uneasy. "Yeah. Sometimes he touches me, you know, down there," she added.

Beth stopped eating. "That's yucky. What do you do?"

"Nothing," Maureen answered. "I don't know what to do."

"You've got to tell your mom."

"I can't. I promised Pete I wouldn't. I might get in trouble."

"Then tell somebody else," said Beth.

Maureen thought about it for a while. "What if no one believes me?" she asked.

"You wouldn't lie about a thing like that," said

Beth. "I'd tell until I found someone who did believe me. That's what I'd do."

"Like who?" asked Maureen.

"Like Mrs. Demartino. Or Miss Ruiz, the nurse. Or your aunt. Or my mom. I bet they'd believe you. There are lots of people."

Maureen began to feel a little better. Beth was the best friend anyone could have, she thought.

"I think I'll talk to Mrs. Demartino," she said.

"Good," said Beth. "I'll go with you and wait outside."

The next day Maureen stayed after school to talk to her homeroom teacher. She told Mrs. Demartino that she didn't like to be alone with Pete, her stepfather.

"Why not?" asked Mrs. Demartino. "Tell me what the problem is."

"It's hard to talk about. Pete said it's a secret. He made me promise not to tell anyone," she said.

"You may feel better if you talk about it," said Mrs. Demartino. "Some secrets shouldn't be kept."

"Well," Maureen said, "sometimes when we're

alone, he touches me in private places. It makes me feel awful."

Mrs. Demartino listened. "You did the right thing, Maureen. It's good that you told me. Your body belongs to you. No one has the right to touch you that way. It's Pete's secret, not yours."

"What can I do about it?" asked Maureen.

"You can say, 'I don't like it when you touch me like that.' But you've already done the most important thing; you've told someone right away. Someone like me who will help you."

"What can you do?" asked Maureen.

"We can't solve this problem alone," explained Mrs. Demartino. "There are people who can help, once we tell them what's been happening."

"Who?" asked Maureen.

"Counselors and other people who look out for and protect children. They will help make Pete stop it, and help him understand that he is wrong. Your mother can help, too. Things will get better, but it will take time." Mrs. Demartino put her arm around Maureen's shoulders. "I'm going to help you, and we'll figure it out together."

Beth was waiting for her on the playground, eating an apple. They walked back through the park, to the baby swings, together.

"I'm glad I talked about it," said Maureen. "I feel better."

Beth smiled. "Want a bite?" she asked. "I want to read you my latest entry."

Maureen took a bite and climbed up on top of one of the little swings to listen.

RESOURCES

WHO I CAN TELL:

Name_____

Address_____

_____

Telephone number_____

WHO I CAN TELL:

Name_____

Address_____

_____

Telephone number_____

American Humane Society, Children's Division
63 Inverness Drive East
Englewood, CO 80112-5117
1-800-227-4645

Childhelp USA National Child Abuse Hotline
1-800-4-A-CHILD

Stop It Now!
P.O. Box 495
Haydenville, MA 01039
1-888-PREVENT

National Clearinghouse on Abuse & Neglect Information
300 C Street SW
Washington, D.C. 20447
1-800-FYI-3366

National Committee to Prevent Child Abuse
332 S. Michigan Avenue, Suite 1600
Chicago, IL 60604
1-312-663-3520